Romancing Your Customer

How to Passionately Attract, Retain, and Win-Back Customers
for Unbelievable Loyalty and Profit

By

Don Williams
CEO, Don Williams Global

Romancing Your Customer

How to Passionately Attract, Retain, and Win-Back Customers for Unbelievable Loyalty and Profit

By

Don Williams

Copyright ©2018 Don Williams

All Rights Reserved

Contact the author at:

1050 W. Pipeline Rd. Suite 103
Hurst, TX 76053-4730
Phone: 800-706-0608
www.alliancedms.com

First Edition

What Others Are Saying

Don Williams is an industry pro that always does right by his clients and customers.
> ~ Jack Wilkie
> President and CEO

Don Williams is a quintessential entrepreneur. Smart, insightful, driven, talented, and a creative wizard, he is genuinely interested in helping others succeed.
> ~ Leslie Hayes
> Leadership Committee
> Entrepreneurs Organization

His pleasant demeanor, clear communication, and vast business experience makes Don Williams the kind of partner you can trust with your business.
> ~ Janis Stevens
> CEO of ITS

Don Williams is the go-to expert on relationship building and sales. Your audience will be enamored by Don's insight, strategies, and stage presence.

~ Allison Maslan
CEO at AMI

Don William's ideas are cutting edge. Don listens and really thinks before he gives an answer.

~ Chiqeeta Jameson
Author, speaker, coach

Dedication

To the brave, creative, and romantic entrepreneurs and business owners that make our lives better.

Table of Contents

How To Use This Book   9

Forward   11

Chapter 1
What is Your Emotional Intelligence?   15

Chapter 2
What is Romance?   30

Chapter 3
Why Should I Romance My Customer?   39

Chapter 4
How Do I Demonstrate Romance?   47

Chapter 5
When Should I Romance My Customer?   56

Chapter 6
Where Should I Romance My Customer?   65

Chapter 7
All Romance, No Sex   71

Chapter 8
Romancing Personal Relationships   81

Chapter 9
Fast Track Tips   92

Chapter 10
Q and A with Don Williams   100

Conclusion   107

Work With Me   109

About the Author   111

How To Use This Book

Romancing Your Customer is an interactive handbook designed to help you passionately attract, retain, and win-back customers for unbelievable loyalty and profit.

Beginning right now!

The margins are wide and there is plenty of white space so you can write notes.

At the end of each chapter are opportunities to immediately put into practice in your business the principles you learned.

Take action by making a plan and working the plan.

Use this book again and again. Each time consider your business, your clients, and fresh ways you can romance your customers with your own brand of the Wow! factor. Create your own style of customer service that reflects appreciation and care for those you work alongside and do business with.

Grab a pen, turn the page, and let's get started romancing to attract, retain, and win-back customers for unbelievable loyalty and profit.

.

Forward

I'm Don Williams and I'll serve as your romance guide through this book. As the founder and CEO of Don Williams Global, my company helps small, medium, and major corporations deliver better experiences to their prospects, which creates loyal and profitable customers.

Have you seen that bumper sticker that says, "I wasn't born in Texas, but I got here as fast as I could"? That's me. I grew up in Kansas and moved to Texas in 1986 when I opened my first company.

During my initial eighteen months in business we nearly starved to death. I did no business. Halfway through that second year, things began to work better and at the end of year two I opened a second location in another city. That second location introduced five more years of struggle, and then in the next three years I transitioned from surviving to thriving in multiple locations.

The single action that resulted in the greatest gain occurred when we, as a company, began looking at everything we did from the customer's point of view.

- How could we help the customer fall in love with our company?

- How could we make doing business with our company such a great experience that our customer looked forward to working with us again?

- How could we add a Wow! factor to our customer service?

The results were astounding. Our company grew from two locations in seven years to 19 locations in three years. Wow! Three years later we pivoted from that company and started a new business.

Since 1999, I've worked with 273 Fortune 500 Companies in marketing, sales and service strategies, and execution. Like Jiminy Cricket, I come alongside the big boys and girls of

American and International business. In addition to my Fortune 500 clients, I've had the great pleasure to work with major firms from Australia, China, France, Greece, Israel, Italy, Spain, United Arab Emirates, and the United Kingdom on efforts in the American and International markets.

One common denominator of major success in businesses from Main Street to Wall Street is – drum roll, please – does a business approach their prospects, customers, and previous customers from an attitude of care and gratitude? Do they show the same appreciation to their employees, contractors, partners, and vendors? In my experience, the great business romantics provide an unparalleled and unforgettable level of service.

Let's look at companies that do a fantastic job romancing their customers and compare how their customer service affects the overall brand of the company, and therefore, the bottom line. This strategy also works with employees, vendors, partners, neighbors, children, and your spouse/mate/love/squeeze. Your customers deserve the rewards of real romance from your company and so do you.

Apply romance liberally for nearly instant results. An added benefit is that you can apply the same principles that make you successful in business to other areas and experience exponential results in your personal life.

Chapter 1

What is Your Emotional Intelligence?

The first time I flew with Emirates Airlines, they sent a driver in a new black Yukon Denali to my home to pick up my wife and me. He drove responsibly, handled our luggage at the baggage counter, and delivered us to our gate in plenty of time to comfortably make our flight.

This first class limo service was included in our business class tickets. With this significant Smash! factor, I felt cared for before we arrived at the airport.

Boarding the airline, a flight attendant greeted me with a smile. "Would you like to see the wine list?"

Surveying the premium wines available, I replied, "I'll have the 2004 Bordeaux, please."

When did you have a ten-year-old wine on an airplane?

After takeoff, another attendant brought a menu offering filet mignon and sea bass. "If you are ready to eat before the time we customarily serve the meal, we can prepare and serve to order."

Dallas / Fort Worth airport to Dubai is a 16-hour flight. After dinner, an attendant asked if I'd like my seat to lie flat like a bed to sleep. Moments later she brought a memory foam mattress complete with high thread count sheets.

Following the best flight I had experienced, we arrived in the busiest airport in the world. Daily, Dubai has more than 90,000 passengers flowing through the airport with the accompanying lines of people needing to get from one place to another. Included in our ticket was a fast pass through customs similar to the express pass at Disneyworld, saving us time and frustration.

Remember the driver who started this story? Another driver in a shiny Mercedes met us at midnight when our plane landed. This driver delivered these weary travelers to the comfort of our hotel. Our return flight from Dubai to the United States proved to be a mirror experience to our exceptional outgoing trip. Wow!

Talk about romancing your customer. No wonder Emirates Airlines is the largest airline in the Middle East and the fourth largest airline by scheduled revenue worldwide.

Romance makes sense. Romance makes dollars, too.

Degree in Romance

Emirates Airlines had a finger on the pulse of what their customers thought and what they liked. With that information in hand, the company established customer service norms that go above and beyond meeting the needs and preferences of their travelers. This strategy resulted in happy flyers that return to do business again and again, and who recommend the airline to others.

The business world has a fanatical love of people with degrees.

- A Ph.D. beats an MBA

- An MBA beats a Masters

- A Masters beats a Bachelors

The system resembles a game of rock/paper/scissors, except you always know who's going to win.

These degrees are respected because they provide trusted standards that indicate a person's ability to learn, practice discipline, complete projects, and consistently improve. Advanced degrees, while not causative, do show a correlation with a higher intelligence.

Think of emotional intelligence as having your Ph.D. in understanding your own feelings, and how you can help others feel valued.

The Power of Emotional Intelligence

Emotional intelligence is the ability to

- Recognize your emotions

- Recognize the emotions others feel

- Discern between different feelings

- Label emotions appropriately

- Use emotional information to guide thinking and behavior

- Manage emotions to adapt to environments

- Adjust your emotions to achieve your goals

Romancing your customer is born in emotional intelligence and then moves through thinking intelligence into action. You must start in your heart, then use your head, and finally get moving with your hands and feet.

Traditional customer experience strategy starts in the brain and then becomes action. The shortfall in that approach is that your customers don't feel your heart.

Businesses generally have a single purpose to make money. Examine any company organization chart, you see the CEO at the top with branches that lead to the most junior staff. What you don't see is a heart.

Making money is a good goal and a worthy purpose. Money is the commodity that allows us to eat well and live indoors, to care for others and ourselves, to fund education, health care, community, and generosity.

When you romance your customer, you increase the value of the business transaction beyond making money. Your personal touch adds respect and honor to both sides of the business relationship.

Improve your customer experience process charts by adding this diagram.

Point of Sale

Follow up Thank you

Two week touch point

Start from Your Heart

If you want to be a big, soft, cuddly, successful romantic and do significantly more business easier, faster, and more efficiently, then start in your heart. You'll attract the right clients and you'll keep them longer.

Most businesses and their customer strategies start in their head or their wallets, and may never reach the heart level.

Heart work is surprisingly easy. Step one is to practice gratitude. Appreciation improves relationships, and at its core, customer service is about the relationship between your company and your customer.

Start today:

- Notice the work your staff performs and say thank you

- Thank your customers for their business

Key Point
Emotional intelligence is the ability to understand your own feelings and help others feel valued.

Action Step
Include the steps above in the heart diagram into your daily business strategy.

- Create a pleasant business experience for your customer

- Follow up with a simple thank you for doing business with you

- In two weeks, contact your customer to see if you can be of further service now or in the future

Customer Log

List ten customers you will call this week.

1.

2.

3.

4.

5.

6.

7.

8.

9.

10.

Jot down a short script you will say to your customer, thanking them for their business.

Script notes:

Mark your calendar to call these ten customers again in two weeks. Jot down a short script you will say, asking if there is anything you can do for them.

Script notes:

Record a few words of feedback from each customer.

1.

2.

3.

4.

5.

6.

7.

8.

9.

10.

Based on the customer feedback you received, is there an action step you can include to improve the romance in your customer service?

Chapter 2

What is Romance?

One of the nation's top ten merchant service companies had a 20 percent annual attrition rate when they came to me for help.

Merchant service companies process credit and debit card transactions for banks and merchants across the country. This group did processing for more than a quarter-million businesses.

My company developed a simple strategy to reduce their high attrition. Each month we personally contacted ten percent of their customers. This is what we said:

"Hello, Mr. Customer, this is XYZ Company. We process your credit cards. First, I want to thank you. We appreciate your business and we're happy to be your credit card processor."

Receiving a phone call to say thank you is enough to shock a lot of businesses. During normal business transactions, it is a rare company that has the good manners to say thank you at the point of transaction to customers who are making purchases.

And we took this gesture to the next level. "While I have you on the phone, is there anything I could do for you? Is your equipment in proper order? Are you hearing from your account exec as often as you would like?"

The majority of those phone calls were answered with, "Wow! I'm all good." Occasionally we talked with a customer that said, "My rep hasn't called me back and I'm out of supplies."

Our reply was, "No problem. I'm entering a trouble ticket now, and you'll hear from a service specialist in 24 hours."

My client had the good manners to follow up within 24 hours. Romance is doing what you say you are going to do.

Some four years later, the client discontinued the program. "You've done a great job and we appreciate you. Because our attrition has gone from 20 percent plus annually to a single digit, we no longer need the program."

By providing romance in the form of good intentions and treating people the way I like to be treated, the results showed up in dollars and cents on my client's bottom line. My company successfully worked ourselves out of a job by helping the client maintain 95 percent of the business they sell, year after year. All because of a little romance.

What Exactly is Romance?

Romancing your customer is creating a Wow! factor that makes doing business with your company an exceptional experience for your client. When your level of customer care – or romance – is memorable, customers are eager to work with you, and they will tell others about your company.

MerriamWebster.com describes romance as

... an emotional attraction or aura belonging to an especially heroic era, adventure, or activity ...

Google says romance is

... a feeling of excitement and mystery associated with love... love, passion, ardor, adoration, devotion; more affection, fondness, attachment, "their romance blossomed"

Romance is Learned

As a man born in Kansas in the 1960s, I'm fairly certain I arrived without the romance gene. But I learned to be romantic. The learning curve felt like a struggle at times, confusing at others, but the efforts were never without positive consequence.

Love is more than feeling. Love is a verb, an action word. Feelings of romance stir romantic thoughts and romantic thoughts become romantic actions.

Romance is more than intimacy. Whether you are talking about personal or business relationships, romance includes ebb and flow, and building a solid, trusted foundation.

Finding Romance

- If you want to find out what your prospects want, just ask.

- If you want to find out what your customers want, just ask.

Asking works with your mate, kids, vendors, partners, employees, coworkers, and neighbors.

When you want to know fast what your customers think and want, call and do a survey over the phone.

Polls and surveys are tools of active listening, designed to collect answers straight from the target audience. Great communication is actually good listening. A company that regularly polls or surveys their customers is in touch with what their customers think, want, and need.

Possible questions to ask your customers include:

- How did we do?

- How can we improve customer service?

- How can we better meet your needs?

- How can we better serve you?

Key Point
To know what your customer thinks and what your customer wants, just ask.

Action Step
Whether you use a survey, phone call, or face-to-face meeting, ask your customer what they need.

To have a professional develop and execute your survey, visit my team at www.alliancedms.com.

Collect Feedback

What information do you want your customers to share with you?

1.

2.

3.

What method will you use to collect this data?

- Face-to-face meeting?

- Telephone poll?

- Email survey?

- Have a professional, such as Alliancedms.com, develop and execute your survey. Contact my team at www.alliancedms.com.

What is the time frame when you will execute your survey?

Begin date:

End date:

Chapter 3

Why Should I Romance My Customer?

Southlake Jewelers is an independently owned jewelry store located in Southlake, Texas. I have known the owner, Jim Bob Baker, for 30 years. Jim Bob owns the business with his brother, Bill. As a family business, at one time or another I think all of their kids, spouses, and long lost cousins have worked in the store.

Southlake is an affluent area of Dallas / Ft. Worth, and their independent business competes against most of the big chain jewelers with recognized names. Here's why Jim Bob is one of my favorite customer romantics.

My brother-in-law, Kurt, lives in Wichita. He and my sister raised three great sons. About a week before Christmas, I was in California attending a $2,500 per day seminar when Kurt sent a text saying my nephew, Dillon, planned to propose

to his girlfriend at Christmas. In preparation for
the grand event, Dillon was shopping for rings at
a big name store in Kansas.

I sent a text asking about color, clarity, and if
the center stone was certified. With those
details in hand, I asked Dillon to hold off for a
minute or two on the final purchase until Uncle
could see if he could help.

Still sitting in the conference, I sent a text to Jim
Bob who responded that he could provide a GIA
Certified diamond of the same quality as the big
name store that was selling a non-certified
stone.

Of course my nephew didn't want to buy a big
diamond he hadn't seen. On the Tuesday before
a Sunday Christmas, Dillon drove to Texas to
meet the Southlake staff, see the diamond, and
choose a setting.

Jim Bob met his new customer, Dillon, on
Tuesday and offered a certified diamond in a
custom setting. Dillon selected the diamond.
Southlake manufactured the setting and set the

stone on Wednesday. The custom designed ring shipped out of state overnight on Thursday for safe arrival on Friday for the planned proposal on Saturday.

This level of personal service – or customer romance – delivered a higher quality product for less money on an impossible schedule the week of Christmas. That's pretty romantic.

Southlake Jewelers is a natural at romancing their customers. That's why I've done business with them for three decades and why I didn't hesitate to refer my nephew to these experts in their field.

Worth the Effort

Because Southlake Jewelers consistently romanced their customers with exceptional service, Jim Bob and his family secured custom designs for my family, my brother's family, and now also for my nephew's family.

Customers are people who want to be valued, respected, and needed. Your customers return to do business with you again and again when they know your company appreciates them.

- Romancing your customer can increase your success exponentially.

- Consistently applying the Wow! factor shifted my business from nearly starving to commonly working with Fortune 500 companies and international firms.

When you thoughtfully show your customers that they are important to you, your customers will:

- Like you more – because you created a positive emotional connection

- Feel better – positivity begets positivity, causing a ripple effect

- Buy more – because you make it easy for them to do business with you

- Stay longer – companies, like people, dislike change. Make your customers feel at home and they have a reason to stay loyal

- Refer more customers – people are more apt to refer others to you when you are that outstanding company that people enjoy working with

Key Point
Customers love when you authentically like them for who they are.

Action Step
What service, that is a step above your current customer care, can you provide for your clients?

Compile
Customer Feedback

With the feedback from your customers that you gathered via your survey or poll, you can improve your customer service.

A) Your first survey question was:

1. Primary answer to the question was:

2. Secondary answer to the question was:

3. Tertiary answer to the question was:

B) Your second survey question was:

    1. Primary answer to your second question was:

    2. Secondary answer to your second question was:

    3. Tertiary answer to your second question was:

C) Your third survey question was:

1. Primary answer to your third survey question was:

2. Secondary answer to your third survey question was:

3. Tertiary answer to your third survey question was:

Chapter 4

How Do I Demonstrate Romance?

Paradise Resort is a small luxury vacation place located off the coast of Thailand on Koh Yao Noi Island in the Andaman Sea. After spending a great week in Bangkok with 15 million of our closest Thai friends, my wife and I were ready for a week on an island with no cars and no paved roads at a get-away with maybe 50 rooms.

The scenery was beautifully surreal. We ate our meals on the beach, enjoyed a daily Thai massage, and walked along the coast as we unwound after a busy quarter. Every villa had its own dip pool as well as a shower, tub, and sink outside in a private setting creatively designed to provide a view of the bay, the Sea Mountains, the sunset, and the beach. Paradise certainly lived up to its name.

Each evening the resort hosted happy hour in an open-air beachside club with a palm roof. The sunset event was the only human interaction we had with others during that week.

A local lady named Layla, just like the Eric Clapton song, served as bartender. She took the time to get to know the guests. Considerate of our retreat, she did not overwhelm us but had a genuine smile of welcome when she saw my wife and me. She asked kind, but not prying questions, and listened when we spoke. She remembered the drinks I liked and the ones my wife enjoyed.

The last night of our visit Layla brought my wife a gift of a handmade sari. A local sari of excellent quality fetched 250 baht or $8.00 U.S. currency. The value of the gift – the romance if you will – wasn't in the monetary value, but in the extraordinary level of thoughtfulness and the total surprise.

The average annual wage in Thailand is maybe 10,000 baht. Our bartender invested 2.5

percent of her yearly income into a friendly guest who she had just met. This is equivalent to your $50K per year bartender at the Ritz Carlton giving you a $1,250.00 gift because you were nice to her. Layla is a head-over-heels customer romantic.

Our departing gratuity proved memorable for Layla. Genuine, caring, and vulnerable, Layla's customer romance action occurred first. We responded in kind. I look forward to sending her a copy of this book and letting Layla know she had a profound effect on me and on the way I do business.

The Power of Vulnerability

Layla dared to be vulnerable with her guests. According to clinical psychological researcher with the University of Houston, Dr. Brené Brown, Ph.D., vulnerability is vital to success in business. Leadership is built on courage. If there's no courage, there's no leadership. And courage comes from daring to be vulnerable.

Most companies exhibit bravado but not real

courage. Dr. Brown offered training to the United States Special Forces, arguably some of the most courageous men and women on the planet. When Brené asked Special Force Operators to think of a time when they witnessed courage without vulnerability, no one could recall a single incident.

- Courage comes from vulnerability

- Leadership is a result of courage

To be a leader where your customers are concerned, you first become vulnerable. Vulnerability happens when you enter into a zone where you do not always know or control the outcome.

To truly romance your customer means to be vulnerable and at risk. A company that gamely gives their best service is courageously vulnerable. You make the first move and risk sharing your expertise without any guarantee how you will be received. Your company invites the customer to do business together. The customer can say yes or no to your invitation.

Where To Begin

Four ways to romance your customers that make a big difference and cost next to nothing are:

1) Mind your manners and you'll stand out from the crowd

2) In person, via the phone, email, short message service or text message (SMS), multi-media message (MMS), or smoke signal, say "please"

   - If you please

   - Would you please

   - Please may I ...

3) Say "thank you." You almost cannot say thank you enough.

   - Thank you for the meeting

   - Thank you for buying

- Thank you for being a long term customer with our company

- Thank you for the referral

- Thank you for the good review

- Thank you for the feedback

4) Ask, "How did I do?" Continually get feedback. This also works for employees, partners, vendors, and prospects.

Transparency is key to a great customer relationship. People want and, maybe more importantly, need to know the how and why of your business. Customers want to know how your business processes relate to them.

The more your customer knows, the more comfortable they are. A customer that feels secure with your business is more likely to do more business, stay with you longer, and refer others to your company.

Key Point
Romance is courageous. Courage is the result of daring to be vulnerable.

Action Step
Practice gratitude.

- Say "thank you" to your customers, vendors, and employees

- Join a Facebook gratitude group

Visit
www.thewowowwowexperience.com
or
www.donwilliamsglobal.com/one-good-thing

Improve Romance
With Customer Feedback

In previous exercises you have:

- conducted a survey or poll

- asked your clientele about their customer experience

- received feedback regarding how your company can better romance your customers

Based on your findings, what three actions can you implement to improve customer romance?

1)

2)

3)

Of these three, which one action will you implement first?

*

Chapter 5

Where Do I Romance My Customer?

About ten years ago, one of my companies, Alliance, helped a client generate leads and offer proposals for trade show displays that ranged in price from $500,000 to one million. Our contact center performed lead generation for several years, providing the high standard of customer care that we always do. Throughout our time working together, we consistently under promised and over delivered.

Two years after our engagement with the trade show display company, Alliance received a call from one of the decision makers from that previous campaign. Now the president of a firm that staffs Locum Tenens Physicians, he wanted a proposal drawn up and contract sent right over. This was the easiest sale of my life.

This company president remembered our

company, and our brand, because of his previous dealings with us. Years later, in a different geographical place, working in another job in a new industry, he thought of our company when he needed a similar service based on the excellent results we had delivered previously.

Effective Communication = Romance

Wherever his career takes him, I think we will continue to work with this gentleman. Proving that we will provide what we say we will, when we say we will, and in a manner that is unparalleled is one way we romance our customers.

In the 1960s, Professor Albert Mehrabian, and his colleagues of the University of California, Los Angles (UCLA), conducted studies into human communication patterns. Their research concluded that the highest quality communication mode is face-to-face. Audio communication, or voice-to-voice ranked second followed by the printed word. Interestingly, the non-verbal aspect, or body language, included in face-to-face and video interactions provides nuances that audio and text do not include. [1]

The Pyramid of Quality Communication

Face to Face

Audio/Video Telephone Calls

Audio Telephone Calls

Written Communication - Letter, postcard, email, fax, chat, form submission, text, etc.

Does that mean you should only communicate with your customers face-to-face or by video? Certainly not, but these findings prove that we have the opportunity to make the largest

---

[1] Professor Albert Mehrabian, http://www.kaaj.com/psych/

romantic impression when we're face to face, on a video chat, or talking by phone. Applying romance to every method of communication merely invites an intentional level of creativity when using other modes of connecting with customers.

Best Communication Styles to Romance Your Customer

1. Face to Face

2. Audio + Video Calls (Zoom, Skype, Facetime)

3. Audio Telephone Calls

4. All Written Styles

Use Only When the Above List is Not Possible

- Email

- SMS/Text

- Website

- Twitter

- Pinterest

- Snapchat and similar apps

- Bill Boards

- Direct Mail

- Skywriting

- People in sandwich board signs, or waving signs on street corners

Look at every method you use to communicate to prospects and customers. Are you practicing romance as well as you could? Chances are you can make some simple shifts to improve your communication with your clients.

A vital first step is to listen to your customer. Find out who they are, what are their needs, and how can you solve their problems to make their life easier and better.

To further define romance and love as applied to personal relationships, eHarmony did a 2017 poll on persons, ages 18 and older, that were married or in long-term relationships.

Listening to their customers, eHarmony discovered:

- Nearly three out of five people claim to have completely open communication

- Open communication means being emotionally transparent and communicating that transparency to the other party

Key Point
Romancing your customer includes providing what you say you will, when you say you will, and in a manner that is unparalleled.

Action Step
Communicate as often as possible with your

client via the four most effective styles:

1. Face to Face

2. Audio + Video Calls (Zoom, Skype, Facetime)

3. Audio Telephone Calls

4. All Written Styles

Take Action
to Romance Your Customer

- You asked

- Your customers responded

- You analyzed their feedback

- You considered the best next steps

- You selected improvements to implement

The first way you will add romance to your customer service is

_____

1) Romancing your customer begins on or before this date

_____

2) The vital first step to add this romantic gesture to your customer service is

   a.

3) Your three-step implementation process

   a.

   b.

   c.

Chapter 6

When Do I Romance My Customer?

Brad has proven himself to be so trustworthy that I purchased a house I hadn't seen from him after a five-minute phone call.

Monthly, Brad hosts a training event for up to 500 physicians at a time. Even though they're attending for the company, these are Brad's personal clients.

Before the event and during, Brad interacts with the valet, bellhop, front desk personnel, and the wait staff at the hotel where the physicians stay when they are in town. Brad romances his supporting cast members who then help him romance his clients. Brad treats his vendors and their staff so well that they pass on excellent service to the physicians that are guests there.

His clients appreciate the excellent service he

provides. The training they learn in a professional atmosphere without distractions stays with them.

With his flare for networking, Brad shared my name with clients interested in my services, and his clients shared Brad's name with their associates.

Romance Early, Often, and Always

The consummate romantic, Brad has an ever-growing network of great people because he romances everyone he comes into contact with. The result is an ever-growing ripple effect of business for Brad and for those in his circle of influence.

The late, great Zig Ziglar said to close early, close often, and close late. Practice romance with your customers the same way – early, often, late, and I would add, always. Romancing your customer is not a technique, a tip, or a trick - it's a business lifestyle, a mindset that begins with the heart.
Romancing your customer has zero shortcuts

and simply won't work if you're unwilling to put in the effort. Make romancing your customer a priority and a lifestyle as Brad has done, and the results speak for themselves.

Get Romantic

- How can your company practice romantic behavior to your customers?

- What actions can your company do to demonstrate your romantic attention to your customer?

- What do you appreciate about your customer?

- How can you authentically share your appreciation for your customer?

Romantic behavior shows up in actions. There are unlimited ways to add romance to a relationship. Studies from eHarmony show:

- 65% schedule dates

- 59% practice romantic gestures

- 46% give small gifts as tokens of affection

Romantic Gestures

Roses, fancy chocolates, exquisite wine, dinner by candlelight, watching beautiful sunsets, music, notes with carefully chosen messages, as well as small and large gifts are romantic.

Romance involves action. Giving roses, sharing a fine wine, and taking someone to dinner are the stuff of romance. Gesture is important to romance because it's an action.

Occasionally giving a gift is the appropriate gesture of romance. Quality gifts that create a Wow! for your customer include:

- Yeti brand cups and coolers. Yes, there are less expensive brands but your customer knows they are less expensive

- Patagonia brand jackets and vests. Yes, there are less expensive brands but your customer will feel the romance with the superior quality

- Experiences like dinners, spa days, and trips

Key Point
Thoughts without actions are meaningless.
Words without actions are meaningless.
Romance without action does not exist.

Action Step
Make romancing your customer a priority in your business. Incorporate romance as a foundational part of your professional mindset.

Listen To Your Results

Once your improved customer service is operational for three months, listen to the responses from your clients, staff, and sales people.

1) Have attitudes shifted?

2) Is there a rise in repeat business?

3) Are clients referring new business to you?

Chapter 7

All Romance, No Sex

One of my businesses is a call center where we make and take phone calls, answer emails, provide live chat, and SMS communications. In 2002, the federal government passed a federal Do Not Call for consumers, and even though we don't do much consumer work, there's still legislation we pay attention to.

Filling out paperwork for one of my vendors, I checked the wrong box that registered me for the Do Not Call Registry. The expense for that was a salty $7,800. I was unaware of my mistake until my American Express bill arrived.

I called the company, explained my mistake, and asked if we could reverse the action.

"Sorry," was the reply. "But it was your mistake."

I contacted the Federal Trade Commission, who received the $7,800, to see if they would refund my error. The FTC didn't answer their phone.

Next I telephoned American Express and explained the situation. "No problem, Mr. Williams," was their immediate response. "We'll reverse the charge." Their instant customer romance proved unforgettable.

A week later, the FTC returned my call. "We see this request for reversal and have issued the credit."

While the FTC refunded the charge, I hold great appreciation for my American Express who received my call and immediately took care of the problem. They have backed me as their card member since 1989. In return, I charge 95 percent of my expenses to my American Express account. I appreciate American Express almost as much as they care about me.

Romance in Science

- Romancing your customer means elevating customer service to provide an experience so positive that customers return again and again to do business with you

- Romancing your customer happens when doing business with your company is such a great experience that your customers recommend your company to others

The concepts to romancing your customer are found in science.

In Ancient Greece, the Greeks defined eight different types of love. Romance, as applied to customers, is a blend of most of the eight types.

- Eros or Erotic Love. The first kind of love is Eros, named after the Greek god of love and fertility

- Philia or Affectionate Love

- Storge or Familiar Love

- Ludus or Playful Love

- Mania or Obsessive Love

- Pragma or Enduring Love

- Philautia or Self Love

- Agape or Selfless Love

Canadian Psychologist, John Alan Lee, created a color wheel by blending the "flavors of love."

In his book, *Colours of Love: An Exploration of the Ways of Loving*, Lee defined

- three primary

- three secondary

- nine tertiary love styles

Lee described and organized the familiar styles of love into a format similar to the traditional color wheel.

Styles of Love

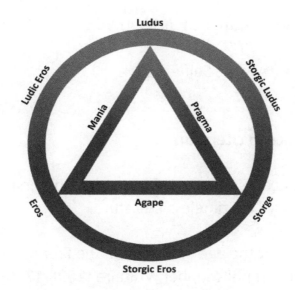

The three primary styles of love are:

- Eros: Erotic Love

- Ludus: Playful Love

- Storge: Familiar Love

The three secondary styles of love are:

- Mania: Obsessive Love

- Pragma: Enduring Love

- Agape: Selfless Love

Romance in Literature

The concepts to romancing your customer are the fodder for timeless literature.

In 1713, at the age of nineteen, the French author and philosopher, Voltaire (1694-1778), traveled to the Netherlands as an attache' to the French Ambassador. While in the Netherlands, he fell in love with French refugee, Catherine Olympe Dunover, the poor daughter of a lower-class woman.

Voltaire's relationship with Olympe did not find favor with his employer or with the girl's mother. In a dramatic move to keep the lovers apart, Voltaire was imprisoned. While in bonds,

Voltaire wrote this passionate letter to his sweetheart.

I am a prisoner here in the name of the King; they can take my life, but not the love that I feel for you. Yes, my adorable mistress, to-night I shall see you, and if I had to put my head on the block to do it ... there is nothing that I will not brave for your sake; you deserve much, more than that. Adieu, my dear heart! [2]

Shortly after, Voltaire escaped by climbing out of the window.

The poet, John Keats, wrote, "I love you the more in that I believe you had liked me for my own sake and for nothing else." [3]

Read the great love stories of history and you'll find tried and proven material to help you formulate your version of romancing your customer.

---

[2] Voltaire - Premium Collection: Novels, Philosophical Writings, Historical Works, Plays, Poems & Letters

[3] Keats (The Letters Of John Keats v.2) 1814-1821

Key Point
Romance is heroic, and includes feelings of mystery and excitement.

Action Step
Invest five minutes to shift your mindset. Close your eyes, take deep slow breaths, and imagine one of the people you love most.

Allow yourself to feel gratitude for this beloved person in your life.

Next, picture yourself mentally "pushing" your love as energy wrapped in thought to that person. Imagine your love, well wishes, and appreciation reaching this person no matter where in the world he or she is located. [4]

---

[4] Thank you, *Gina Mollicone-Long.*

Your Romance Style

Some romance styles come naturally. All styles of romance can be learned.

Consider these styles:

- Affectionate Love

- Familiar Love

- Playful Love

- Enduring Love

- Self Love

- Selfless Love

1) What style comes easy to you?

2) What romance style can you improve?

3) What style can you learn?

4) What romance style is a natural fit for your business?

5) What romance style will have the best impact on your customers who do business with your company?

Chapter 8

Romancing Personal Relationships

In a book about business and how to passionately attract, retain, and win-back customers for unbelievable loyalty and profit, why include a chapter on romancing your personal relationships?

The answer is simple: how you are in *one* area of your life is how you are in *all* areas of your life.

When you are diligent to romance your customers, you will automatically improve your personal relationships as well. When you nurture your personal relationships, it follows that your customer relationships will benefit.

As Zig Ziglar said, "People who have good relationships at home are more effective in the marketplace."

Most Important

The most important and life-giving ingredient for any relationship is respect. In business, we don't always actually choose our customers. Many come because they are seeking a particular service you provide. A strong business is clear on what the company offers and how they can best provide their specialty.

Years ago, marriages were arranged. These relationships were based more on business partnerships than on romance. Arranged marriages, like business partnerships and customer relationships, could thrive when built on a foundation of respect.

Romancing your personal relationships affirms your appreciation and respect for the people in your inner circle.

Show Respect

- Active listening is one of the most romantic gestures you can give

- Listen. People feel heard and respected when you listen to their story

- Family and friends, neighbors and community members want to know their opinion matters. You do not have to agree, but people feel respected when they feel they have been heard

- Most arguments have less to do with who is right and more about each person needing to be heard

- Listen without interrupting

- When you have heard the other person fully, say, "What I heard you say is (and repeat back a summary of what you heard). Did I understand you correctly?"

- Invite the other person to explain their point again until you can repeat back what was said well enough that the other person feels you understand their words correctly

- Realize that what is said is not always what is heard. We can filter what someone says through our own unique experiences

Know Their Heart

Like a good detective, pay attention to what is important to your customers and to your personal relationships.

One newlywed was told that wives appreciate fancy jewelry. For their first anniversary, he gave his wife diamond earrings. She promptly sucked one up in the vacuum. The following year he observed that when she spoke about someday writing a book, her eyes lit up. For their second anniversary, she was overjoyed when he gave her a laptop. Both the diamonds and the computer were lovely gifts. The difference between the jewelry and the laptop was the laptop showed he knew her heart.

Listen with your heart to the hearts of those in your circle of influence.

Just Ask

In Chapter 2: What is Romance, I encouraged you to ask your customer questions like:

- How did we do?

- How can we improve customer service?

- How can we better meet your needs?

- How can we serve you better?

Once you have the feedback, do what you can to improve customer service.

In the same way, ask your close relationships what they need. An effective and relationship-improving question is:

- How can I make your day better?

Then follow through by either doing what was suggested or arrange to have the task done.

New York Times bestselling author, Richard Paul Evans, says his marriage went from dismal to happy and content when he asked his wife each morning, "How can I make your day better?" Once he heard her answer, he followed through to provide results. Initially his wife didn't believe his question was sincere but he remained consistent. The results were more than worth the effort.

Romancing your customer, like romancing your personal relationships, boils down to making their day – and their life – better.

Your interest in the wellbeing of others doesn't need to take all your time. Small gestures make a world of difference and show your important relationships they are appreciated and valued.

- Keep indoor and outdoor maintenance on schedule

- Arrange regular oil changes for your teen's vehicle

- Close your laptop to give your full attention when talking to others

- Turn off the television when conversing with someone

- Be early. If you can't be early, be on time

- Listen without interrupting

- Even when you don't agree, give the gift of hearing the other person's opinion

- Pick up after yourself

Key Point

How you are in one area of your life is how you are in all areas of your life.

Action Step

What can you do today to show respect to your loved ones?

Your Closest Relationships

Friends, family, and neighbors make up your personal relationships.

Too often we trust that those we love the most will be the most forgiving when we short-change our personal relationship in favor of business.

Usually we are aware of a simple act we can do that will show love to those we live life with. Something we have been stubbornly refusing such as

- Turn off the light when leaving a room

- Make a dental cleaning appointment

- Pick up dirty clothes

- Put dishes in the dishwasher

- Call when you will be late

What will you do to romance those you live with?

We say "I love you" to those around us when we practice our own self-care. What can you begin today that supports your best health?

- Drink 8 glasses of water daily

- Take a walk at lunch

- Stop eating for two when no one is eating with you

- Take a vacation

- Get 7 to 8 hours of sleep nightly

Practice vulnerability and courage by asking your loved one

- What can I do to make your day better?

Bonus points if you do what Darren Hardy recommends in his book, *The Compound Effect.* Weekly ask your family

- for a review of their week

- if there is something you can do that would make their life with you better

To the best of your ability, implement those changes that resonate with your heart. You know, the ones that truly would be beneficial to you and those around you.

Notice how your business relationships grow when your personal relationships flourish.

Chapter 9

Fast Track Romance Tips From Don Williams

Entrepreneurs don't know how to quit. They figure it out. At least that's what I did after nearly starving for my first five years in my own business.

This book is a compilation of the smart practices that turned my struggling enterprise into a respected company with international influence.

Everyone is an example. Sometimes we are an example of what to do. Other times we are examples of what *not* to do. This chapter is a quick reference of both recommended principals and a handful of mistakes to avoid. These are the dos and don'ts.

Your Wow! Factor

- Do practice self-care. Treat yourself well so you can treat your staff and clients with respect and appreciation. Creating your unique Wow! factor begins with you.

- Don't skip adequate rest, good nutrition, and seasons of rest and refreshment. These ingredients are key to your health and the wellbeing of your business.

- Do consider publishing a small book that outlines what your company offers. A book serves as your best business card to potential customers, and saves you time explaining your company.

- Don't neglect to share your book with event coordinators and the media. In addition to perceived credibility, your book proves you have resources and material to offer as a coach, speaker, and expert in your field.

- Do hire a qualified writer or marketer to produce a professional book and marketing materials for your company.

- Don't think all seven billion people on the planet are all potential customers for you.

- Do be realistic with your geographic and demographic restrictions. Narrow down your target audience, and focus your marketing to them.

- Don't randomly purchase customer lists. These resources are beneficial only after you know the exact people to market to.

- Do ask the companies that sell customer lists to help you know your most promising prospects.

- Don't waste your time, effort, and money talking to prospects that are outside your target market. Don't sell ice to Eskimos but call them if you sell heaters.

- Do craft a concise script to say that honors your time and the time of your potential client. A powerful script is: "I'm Don Williams, owner of Acme Company. If you need something we provide, or if you know someone who needs what we provide, please call me. Here is my contact number. Thank you."

- Do call a specified number of prospects every week and use the script above. Before long you will have so much business you will no longer need to prospect.

- Don't hesitate to hire someone to make your weekly prospect calls using the script provided above. Then you are free to do business with those who respond.

- Do hire the best talent you can find. Populate your team with people who want to do that job, are a bit competitive, and have an excellent work ethic.

- Do use your telephone to drive business and better serve your customer.

- Don't wait to get your prospecting department fully functional to pursue business. Hire a professional contact center with successful management experience to serve your customers.

- Don't try to do everything yourself. You don't have time to be on the phone with customers all day and run the business. Let the experts with all the updated technology make calls for you until you can get your own marketing and customer service department up and running.

- Do consider which type of outsourcing is the best solution for your goal. Whether contracting with a company in the United States, in another country like Canada, or offshore such as a service in India, each option has advantages.

- Do use updated and current phone technology to better drive business and serve your customers.

- Do create a customer journey map. Track every touch point – or feel point – when you connect with your client. Did each encounter deliver a Wow! experience for your customer?

- Don't forget that one poor experience can wipe out a track record of excellent connections with your customer.

- You may be an expert in your field with a high I.Q. – intelligence quotient. But if your E.Q. – emotional quotient – is not your strong point, hire someone who can do that part of your business for you. Romancing your customer is vital to the success of your business.

- Do solve their problem as one of the best ways to romance your customer. Approach challenges shoulder to shoulder with the intent to resolve the issue together.

- Don't become antagonistic.

- Do speak with a calm and peaceful voice.

- Don't interrupt.

- Do say, "I can help you with that." This is a reassuring phrase when someone has a problem and encourages them to have confidence that you can provide a solution.

- Don't leave your customer floundering if you cannot fix the problem. Instead, take responsibility to find someone who can provide a satisfactory resolution.

- Do follow up with the customer to be certain the issue is taken care of to the customer's satisfaction.

Your Fast Track Romance Tips

Developing your business, you've discovered actions that work and ones that don't.

Your knowledge is valuable to

- train workers

- mentor new business owners

- share at high school and college business classes

- present workshops to the Chamber of Commerce

- speak at industry associations

List your own dos and don'ts.

Chapter 10

Q & A

Q: What is the most economical, efficient, and effective way to gain loyal customers?

A: Romancing your customer provides the

- easiest acquisition

- lowest cost per acquisition

- highest lifetime value

- longest customer lifecycle

- ability to win back a customer when they leave

Romancing your customer means elevating customer service through a love language to the level of customer experience.

Q: What is a love language?

A: Generally, people give and receive love according to five styles. Gary Chapman identified these love languages as

- words of affirmation

- gifts

- touch

- service

- quality time

Q: How can my company incorporate the love languages into our customer service?

A: As recommended in chapters one and four, words of affirmation include saying thank you. Let your customers know you appreciate doing business with them.

Chapter six talks about giving gifts as part of your customer service experience.

Making eye contact, smiling warmly, and shaking hands when you meet your clients face-to-face is a way to provide appropriate and respectful touch.

Service is the most natural of the love languages. Set the industry standard by consistently providing excellent service.

Chapter one gives a step-by-step mechanism to romance your clients through the love language of quality time.

- Create a pleasant business experience for your customer

- Follow up with a simple thank you for doing business with you

- In two weeks, contact your customer to see if you can be of further service now or in the future

Q: Where do you find inspiration to romance your customers?

A: When you are enjoying life, having fun with your work, and pursuing fulfilling interests and relationships, the inspiration to create quality experiences for your customers flows naturally.

Q: How do you inspire good attitudes in your staff?

A: Weekly, the staff at my company gathers for leadership meetings. We begin by sharing something we are thankful for. Practicing gratitude develops good attitudes.

Q: What makes strong leaders?

A: Strong leaders support and care for their staff so their staff can romance the company's customers. Strong leaders are courageous to be vulnerable.

Q: What are quick ways a company can immediately begin to romance their customers?

A:

- Deliver your product or service before you promised

- Practice good manners

- Say please

- Say thank you

- Listen to really hear what your customer says

Q: How can I practice romance everyday?

A:

- Learn the names of people you encounter from the flight attendant to the taxi driver to the receptionist

- Make eye contact

- Invite someone to go first in line

- Pay for the other person's meal

- Remember a birthday

- Be polite

- Open doors for others

- Smile

- Write a thank you note

- Listen without interrupting

- Leave a generous tip

Your Questions

As questions arise, write them here.

Smart entrepreneurs always have an intelligent question or two immediately available for those serendipitous opportunities when you have a chance to talk with an expert.

Conclusion

Shakespeare's *Romeo and Juliet* is the romance between two people who felt they couldn't, and wouldn't, live without the other. If your company is going to have that Romeo and Juliet type of business/customer care affair, you'll have to add romance to the mix.

1. Romance is courageous

2. Romance is heroic

3. Romance includes feelings of mystery and excitement

4. Romance means being vulnerable

Whether you're a

- Solopreneur

- Entrepreneur

- Fortune 500 CEO

my hope is that you become a hopeless customer romantic. Your customers deserve it and so do you.

Now go and romance your customer!

Work With Me

Want to take your business to the next level?

Get equipped with proven tools for success. Educational and entertaining, Don Williams delivers cutting edge insights that help you and your team become industry leaders.

Learn how to quickly implement exceptional customer service in your specific market to passionately attract, retain, and win back loyal customers.

Schedule Don to speak at your next event.
Call the Don Williams team at 800-823-0403.
Or email speaking@donwilliamsglobal.com

Want Explosive Growth?

Do you want explosive growth fast?

Many businesses are one or two simple steps from explosive growth. Don Williams

- tripled his business in only three days by implementing a new strategy that cost exactly nothing

- increased a client's revenue by 50 percent in just four hours

And Don can customize a strategy to turn your remarkable service into powerful profits.

If you want big, crazy, mammoth, gigantic, and fast results, schedule strategic consulting with Don Williams.

Call the Don Williams team at 800-823-0403. Or email consulting@donwilliamsglobal.com

About The Author

Don Williams and his companies run campaigns and consult with businesses worldwide to develop and execute Wow! customer experiences. Don opened his first company in 1986 and founded a dozen other successful firms. With hundreds of repeat clients, Don's contact center business, Alliance, has been an industry standard in the professional services niche since 1999. Don lives in the Dallas / Ft. Worth, Texas area with the love his life, Leta, and their three chocolate Labrador retrievers.